My Sc
school trip

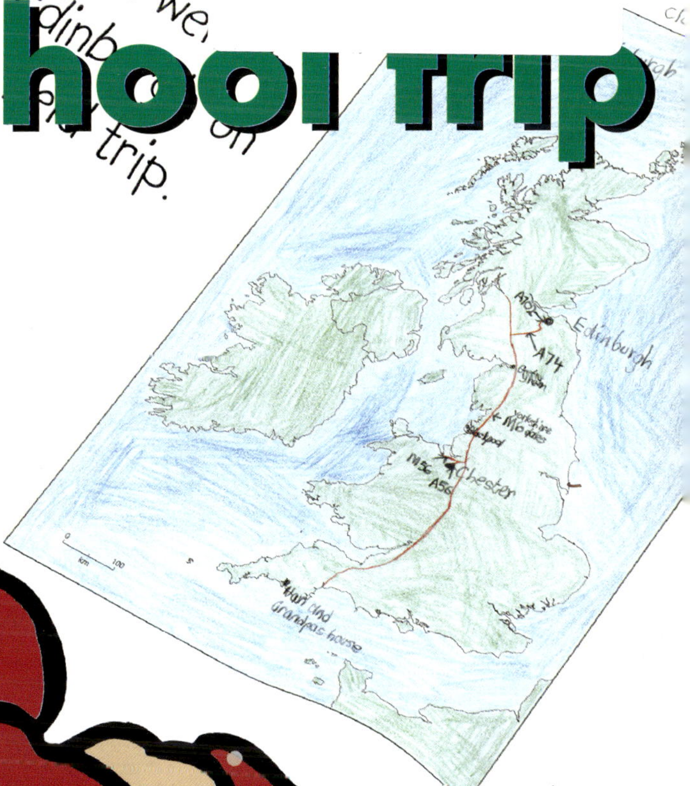

Liz Lewis

Geographical Association

On Monday our class went to Edinburgh on a field trip.

We stayed at a Youth Hostel.

Photo: Robert Day

On Tuesday we climbed a big hill called Arthur's Seat

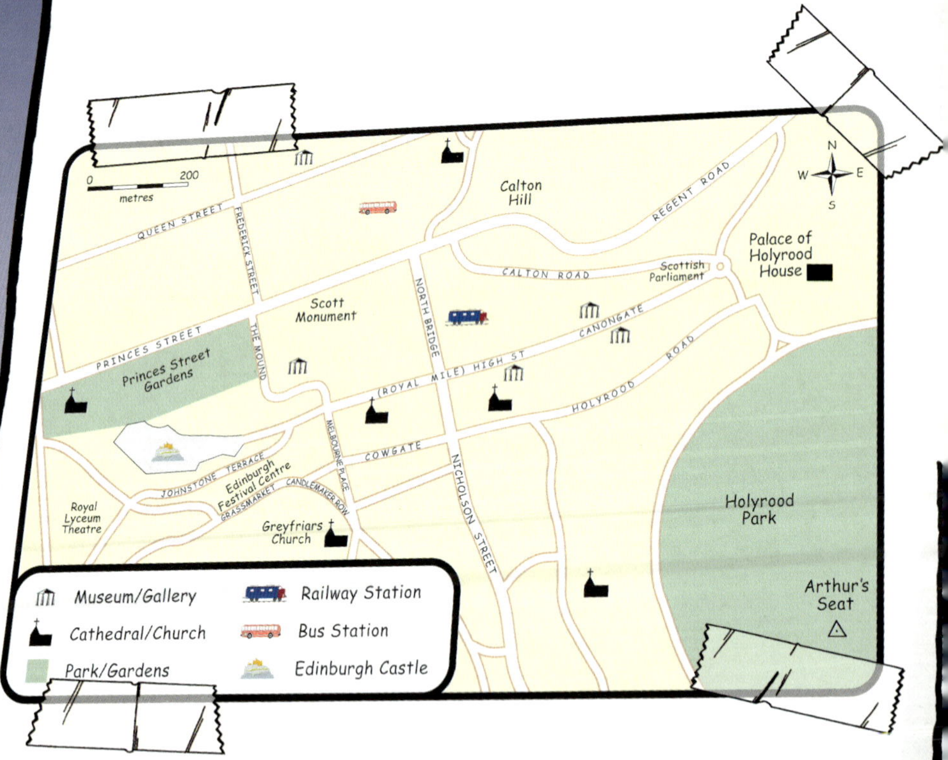

From the top we could see a long way across the city.

Photo: Margaret Mackintosh

On Wednesday we went to the castle.

heard a man playing bagpipes.
Photo: Elaine Jackson

On Thursday
we went shopping
and had a picnic
in the park.

The palace flag only flies when the Queen is there.

Photos courtesy of Edinburgh and Lothians Tourist Board/Harvey Wood, Douglas Corrance and Marius Alexander

On Friday
we drew field
sketches in the old streets.

Photo: S.J. Taylor/Still Moving Picture Company

We heard the story about a dog called Bobby.

Photo: Elaine Jackson

The best bit was when we saw the two huge bridges.

Photo: Doug Corrance/Still Moving Picture Company